104/55
4.3
0.5
No Lexile

D1369599

Questions and Answers: Physical Science

Light

A Question and Answer Book

by Adele Richardson

Consultant:
Philip W. Hammer, PhD
Vice President, The Franklin Center
The Franklin Institute Science Museum
Philadelphia, Pennsylvania

Capstone press
Mankato, Minnesota

Fact Finders is published by Capstone Press,
151 Good Counsel Drive, P.O. Box 669, Mankato, Minnesota 56002.
www.capstonepress.com

Library of Congress Cataloging-in-Publication Data
Richardson, Adele, 1966–
    Light: a question and answer book / by Adele Richardson.
    p. cm.—(Fact finders. Questions and answers. Physical science)
    Summary: "Introduces light's sources, components, forms, and movement, as well as
humans' perception of light"—Provided by publisher.
    Includes bibliographical references and index.
    ISBN-13: 978-0-7368-5446-7 (hardcover)
    ISBN-10: 0-7368-5446-0 (hardcover)
    ISBN-13: 978-1-4296-0224-2 (softcover pbk.)
    ISBN-10: 1-4296-0224-4 (softcover pbk.)
    1. Light—Juvenile literature. I. Title. II. Series.
QC360.R528 2006
535—dc22   2005020125

Editorial Credits
Chris Harbo, editor; Juliette Peters, designer; Molly Nei and Tami Collins, illustrators;
    Jo Miller, photo researcher; Scott Thoms, photo editor

Photo Credits
Capstone Press/Karon Dubke, 19, 21, 23, 24, 25, 29 (all)
Corbis/Brian A. Vikander, 18; Clayton J. Price, cover; Gabe Palmer, 20; Mark Gamba, 16;
    zefa/Nation Wong, 17
Digital Vision Ltd., 8
Folio Inc./Fredde Lieberman, 27
Fundamental Photographs/Paul Silverman, 13; Richard Megna, 1
Getty Images Inc./Mario Villafuerte, 15
The Image Finders/Eric R. Berndt, 5
Index Stock Imagery/Creative Concept, 10; Diaphor Agency, 26
Photo Researchers Inc./Darwin Dale, 6; Gregory Ochocki, 22; Laurent/Carola, 14
UNICORN Stock Photos/Dinodia, 4; Mark E. Gibson, 9
Visuals Unlimited/Tom Walker, 12

Table of Contents

Features

What is light?

Have you ever watched the sun rise? As it moves up in the sky, the land begins to glow. Trees, buildings, and animals once hidden in the dark can suddenly be seen. The sun's light shows us the world around us.

The sunrise reveals palm trees along a tropical beach at dawn.

Light allows us to see the books we read.

Light is a form of **energy**. It travels through space and passes through many things, like windows. It heats up a room on a sunny day, and it helps us find our way in the dark. Light is an important form of energy the whole planet needs.

Where does light come from?

The sun, a lightbulb, and fire all have something in common. They are all hot and produce light. Much of the light we see comes from things that are hot, but not all of it. Fireflies glow because chemicals in their bodies produce light. Whether made by heat or chemical reaction, all light is created in **atoms**. What are atoms? They are the tiny particles that make up everything around us.

A firefly uses a chemical reaction in its body to make light.

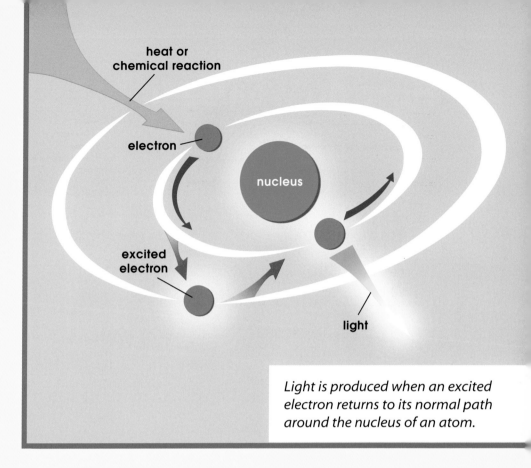

Light is produced when an excited electron returns to its normal path around the nucleus of an atom.

Atoms produce light with their **electrons**. Electrons are tiny particles that circle the center of the atom. When heat or a chemical reaction affects an electron, it gains energy and gets excited. The electron jumps to a path farther from the atom's center. Eventually, the electron loses energy and returns to its normal path. We see the energy loss as light.

How do we use light?

Light is always part of your life. Besides needing sunlight outdoors, people depend on light to work and live indoors. Electricity in office buildings and shopping malls provides light for businesses day and night. The lightbulbs in our lamps let us read long after the sun goes down.

Fact!

Satellites in space use solar panels to collect light from the sun. They turn the sunlight into the power they need to run.

Crops such as corn need sunlight to live and grow.

But we need light for more than just finding the bathroom in the middle of the night. We need light for food too. Plants use sunlight to live and grow. Without it, plants couldn't grow the fruits and veggies we eat.

Some people use sunlight to make **solar energy**. Solar panels collect sunlight and change it into electricity people use.

What do waves have to do with light?

All light travels in waves similar to the waves in the ocean. Like ocean waves, light waves can be measured in **wavelengths**. A wavelength is the distance between the tops of two waves next to each other.

Fact!

Light travels at about 186,200 miles (299,650 kilometers) per second. That's fast! Still, many stars in the night sky are so far away their light takes thousands of years to reach the earth.

Electromagnetic Spectrum

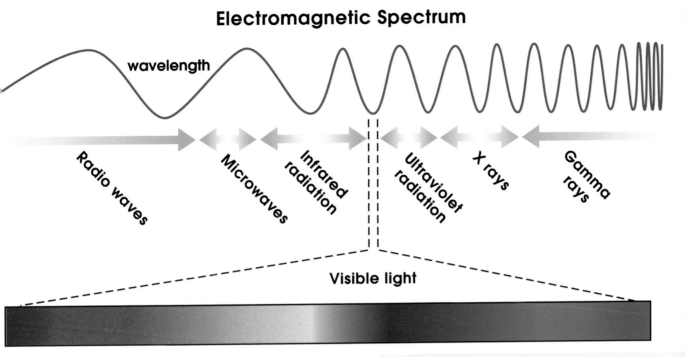

The colors red, orange, yellow, green, blue, indigo, and violet are the only part of the electromagnetic spectrum people can see.

Sunlight travels to the earth in different wavelengths. Together, these wavelengths make up the **electromagnetic spectrum**. Most light has wavelengths that are too short or too long to see. Your eyes can only see light with certain wavelengths. The shortest wavelengths you can see look violet. The longest wavelengths you can see look red.

Why do rainbows sometimes appear?

For a rainbow to appear, the weather must be just right. First, the sun must be shining behind you. Second, rain needs to be falling in the distance in front of you. If these two things are happening, you might see a rainbow. Why? Because the sunlight **refracts**, or bends, when it shines on raindrops. As it bends, the light splits into colors.

A rainbow forms when raindrops bend sunlight.

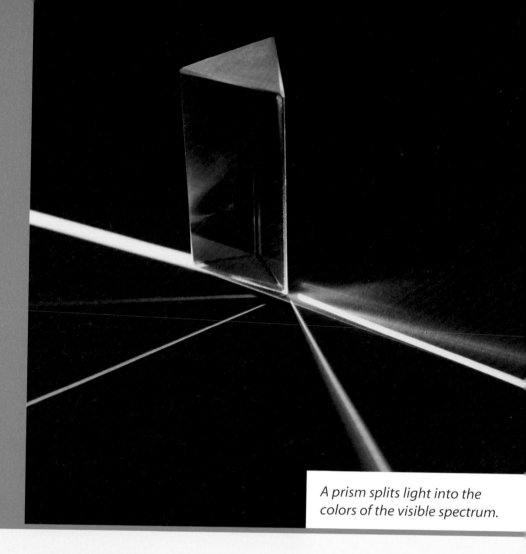

A prism splits light into the colors of the visible spectrum.

Raindrops that make rainbows act just like **prisms**. A prism is any object that refracts light passing through it. Although sunlight looks white, it's made up of all the other colors of the visible spectrum. A prism splits white light into the colors we see in a rainbow.

What causes sunburns?

Sunburns are caused by light we can't see. Our eyes can only see the light waves from red to violet on the light spectrum. But just beyond violet are even shorter waves. These waves are called **ultraviolet light**. The sun gives off a lot of ultraviolet light. These short light waves cause sunburns.

Fact!

Sunburns happen faster than you think. On a sunny summer day, your skin can burn in as little as 15 minutes.

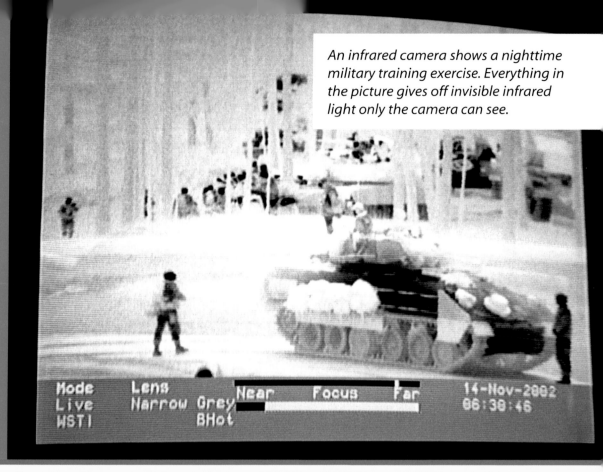

An infrared camera shows a nighttime military training exercise. Everything in the picture gives off invisible infrared light only the camera can see.

Mode   Lens   Near   Focus   Far   14-Nov-2002
Live   Narrow Grey   06:30:46
WST1   BHot

Ultraviolet light is not the only light we can't see. Just beyond red on the spectrum is **infrared light**. We feel this kind of light as heat. Anything that releases heat gives off infrared light—even your body. The military uses infrared cameras to see a person's body heat. These cameras let soldiers see in total darkness because they can see infrared light.

Why do some things make shadows?

Some things will not let light pass through. When light hits these objects, shadows form. A shadow is really an outline of the object the light hit. Material that does not let light pass through is **opaque**. Wood, brick, and even your body are opaque. They all block light and make shadows.

On a bright, sunny day our bodies cast shadows of our movements.

16

A cat spies a fish through the transparent glass and water.

Other materials let light pass through. These things are **transparent**. While they block some light, most light passes right through them. You can tell if something is transparent because you can see through it. Glass and water are transparent materials.

How does the moon light up at night?

The moon does not produce its own light. It's just a rock in space. But sunlight that hits the moon **reflects**, or bounces, off its surface. After bouncing off the moon, the light travels to the earth and our eyes.

The moon gets its glow from the light it reflects from the sun.

You can see the words in a book because light reflects off the pages.

Everything we see reflects light—even you. That's why we see the grass in our backyards and the buildings in our cities. Right now, light is reflecting off the pages of this book. If it didn't, you wouldn't be able to see it to read it.

Why do the words on my shirt look backward in a mirror?

As we know, all objects we can see reflect light. But some objects reflect light better than others. Mirrors are very flat and shiny. Light that hits them from one direction bounces off in the exact opposite direction.

Fact!

Why is the word "ambulance" spelled backward on the front of an ambulance? Because drivers sometimes see ambulances rush up behind them in their rearview mirrors. Drivers see the word spelled forward in their mirrors.

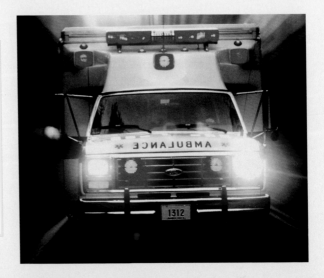

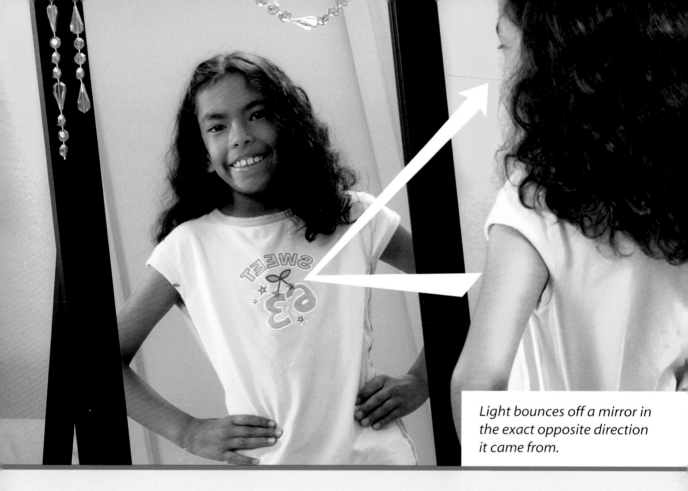

Light bounces off a mirror in the exact opposite direction it came from.

If you could see light's path, it would look like the letter "V" on its side. This path makes things look backward in the mirror. The image we see is the exact opposite of the object in front of the mirror. We read from left to right. But in a mirror, the words run from right to left.

Why does a straw look broken in a glass of water?

A straw looks broken because light refracts when it passes through different transparent materials. The water, the glass, and the air around the glass are all transparent. Light that passes through more than one transparent material bends several times.

Fact!

Light moves through water at about 139,800 miles (225,000 kilometers) per second. At that speed, a wave of light could circle the earth more than five times in one second.

The water and glass bend light so that the straw looks broken.

Light travels fast through air. When it passes through water, it slows down. It also changes direction. When light passes through glass, it slows down and changes direction a little more. All the slowing down and changing directions bends the light. The straw looks broken because light reflecting off of it bends more below the water than above the water.

Why does the street get hotter than the sidewalk?

Have you noticed how a blacktop street feels hotter than a concrete sidewalk on a sunny day? The reason is because dark colors **absorb**, or soak up, a lot of light's energy. Lighter colors reflect more light. The street feels hotter because its dark surface soaks up light. The sidewalk stays cooler because its gray color reflects more light.

A blacktop street absorbs more light than a concrete sidewalk. The street feels hotter when you step on it.

On a sunny day, the fur on a black dog feels warmer than the fur on a light brown dog.

The colors you wear on a sunny day make a big difference in how hot you feel. A black shirt feels hotter than a white one because it absorbs more light. But at least you can change shirts if you get too hot.

Your pets aren't so lucky. A black dog's fur feels a lot hotter than a lighter dog's fur on a sunny day.

Why can cats see better in the dark than people can?

People and cats both need light to see. But people can't see as well in the dark. Try putting your face close to a mirror. Cup your hands on the sides of your eyes. Slowly take your hands away. Watch the tiny black circles in your eyes. They are pupils. They get smaller when light gets brighter. In the dark, pupils get bigger to let in more light.

People have round pupils. On a bright day, the pupils shrink to let less light into the eyes.

A cat's pupils look like oval slits. In the dark, these slits open very wide to let in more light.

A cat's pupils are not round. They look like slits. The slits open much wider in the dark than the round pupils of people. So cats get more light into their eyes.

Fast Facts about Light

- The sun's light and heat can be made into electricity.

- Light travels about 6 trillion miles (9.5 trillion kilometers) through outer space in a year. This distance is called a light year.

- The colors of the visible light spectrum blend together to make white light.

- Dark colors absorb more light than lighter colors.

- Fluorescent lightbulbs give off small amounts of ultraviolet light.

- A prism is an object that refracts, or bends, light passing through it.

- A shadow is an outline of something that light hits but cannot pass through.

- Cats see better than humans in the dark because their eyes take in more light.

- Each color of light we see is a different wavelength.

Hands On: Bouncing Light

Light travels in a straight line until it hits something that changes its direction by reflection or refraction. Try this experiment to see how reflection can bounce light around a room.

What You Need

masking tape   *table*
paper towel tube   *small mirror*
flashlight
dark room

What You Do

1. *Tape one end of the paper towel tube to the lightbulb end of the flashlight.*
2. *Turn off all of the lights in the room and turn on the flashlight.*
3. *Place the flashlight on one end of the table.*
4. *Set the mirror on the other end of the table. Hold up the mirror so the flashlight shines on it.*
5. *Watch where the light goes.*

Can you see the light from the flashlight moving around on the wall? The beam of light reflects off the shiny, flat mirror. It bounces back toward the flashlight and hits the wall behind it. Try the experiment again, but this time change the angle of the mirror. See if you can get the beam of light to shine on the ceiling or the floor. How many directions can you send the beam of light?

Glossary

absorb (ab-ZORB)—to soak up

atom (AT-uhm)—an element in its smallest form

electromagnetic spectrum (i-lek-troh-mag-NET-ik SPEK-trum)—all of the wavelengths of light

electron (i-LEK-tron)—a tiny particle in an atom that travels around the nucleus

energy (EN-ur-jee)—the ability to move things or do work

infrared light (IN-fruh-red LITE)—light that produces heat; humans cannot see infrared light.

opaque (oh-PAYK)—blocking light

prism (PRIZ-uhm)—a transparent object that bends light

reflect (ri-FLEKT)—to bounce light off the surface of an object

refract (ri-FRACT)—to bend light as it passes through a substance at an angle

solar energy (SOH-luhr EN-uhr-jee)—heat or electricity that is made from light from the sun

transparent (transs-PAIR-uhnt)—letting light through

ultraviolet light (uhl-truh-VYE-uh-lit LITE)—light from the sun that people cannot see; ultraviolet light causes sunburns.

wavelength (WAYV-length)—the distances between the peaks of a wave

Internet Sites

FactHound offers a safe, fun way to find Internet sites related to this book. All of the sites on FactHound have been researched by our staff.

Here's how:
1. Visit *www.facthound.com*
2. Type in this special code **0736854460** for age-appropriate sites. Or enter a search word related to this book for a more general search.
3. Click on the **Fetch It** button.

FactHound will fetch the best sites for you!

Read More

Cooper, Christopher. *Light: From Sun to Bulbs.* Science Answers. Chicago: Heinemann, 2004.

Hunter, Rebecca. *The Facts About Light.* Science, The Facts. North Mankato, Minn.: Smart Apple Media, 2005.

Stille, Darlene R. *Light.* Science Around Us. Chanhassen, Minn.: Child's World, 2005.

Trumbauer, Lisa. *All About Light.* Rookie Read-About Science. New York: Children's Press, 2004.

Index